C000122288

ALBERT EINS

A Life From Beginning to End

Copyright © 2017 by Hourly History

All rights reserved.

Table of Contents

Introduction

Creativity was the fuel which sparked life as we know it. Some say it's more important than intelligence. Others speak of it as the catalyst for our very being. It is what makes us human. Lower animals don't have creativity; they rely on patterns and what is ingrained in their species.

If ever there was a human being who defines the idea of creativity it would have to be Albert Einstein. From the frizzy, wild hair to those twinkling eyes which seemed so alive, to his way of engaging students and scientists alike, Einstein was blessed with an imagination that lit up not only his world but would set the world on fire with ideas and realities never before seen.

The modern era could be said to have begun in Albert Einstein. Without him immigrating to the United States, much of his work would have laid undiscovered. It was his passion for freedom that set his mind alight. Combining that with all that his imagination would provide him, Einstein literally opened up new horizons and universes to the world.

The world was about to change when Einstein was born. He stood along with everyone else on the precipice of a time in history which would rival no other. Grand things were coming.

Albert Einstein believed that harmony was the foundation of the laws of the universe. His life work would be to unlock the mechanics behind the harmonious facade. He would only do this by breaking free of conformist thought; by letting his imagination think beyond the present.

Einstein would envision it all. From the infinite to the finite, from nuclear power to fiber optics, from semiconductors to space travel, from supernovas to atom bombs, his face would become one of the most recognizable in history. His life would truly mirror all that creativity and imagination can do for any one person.

Before Einstein, the universe and all its powers seemed beyond human understanding. Because of the wit and wisdom of this remarkable man, much of deep space was lassoed in to be taught and understood in all its glory. Come along to see what made Albert Einstein tick.

Chapter One

Early Life

"I have no special talents. I am only passionately curious."

—Albert Einstein

When Albert Einstein was born, Germany had been a country for nine short years. For centuries, Germany had been a collection of nation-states, little principalities, free cities, and small duchies. It wasn't until a new chancellor known as Otto von Bismarck was elected that he finally united the German regions into one country.

In one of these areas, called Swabia, lived the Einstein family. Albert was born in the city of Ulm, which lay in the Baden-Württemberg region of southwest Germany, on the Danube River. This Swabia region was known to be the home of many Jewish settlements.

Einstein's parents were Hermann Einstein, a salesman and engineer, with a keen interest in mathematics, and Pauline Koch. His parents were married in 1876, and on March 14, 1879, Albert first saw the light of day. The following year, the family moved to Munich, where Einstein's father and uncle founded a small company which manufactured electrical current.

In his early years, Einstein was a quiet baby. He spoke not a single word. This puzzled and worried his parents, and it wasn't until a younger sister, Maria, nicknamed Maja, was born two years later, that the young Einstein began talking.

Today, there are those who have speculated that Einstein may have been autistic. However, when he died in 1955, and his brain was dissected, it was found that the parietal lobes in his brain were at least fifteen percent larger than the average person's; leading to a cautious conclusion that he did not suffer from autism, as autistic people have smaller parietal lobes in their brains.

Whether or not Albert Einstein had a lot to say in his toddler years, by the time he was five years old, he was enrolled in a Catholic elementary school in Munich, Germany. His parents were Jewish but did not observe or go to the temple. Einstein remained in the Catholic school for three years, when he was transferred to the Luitpold Gymnasium. He was enrolled here for the next seven years. Little did he know, that the school would later be renamed to Albert Einstein Gymnasium.

In 1894, Hermann Einstein and his brother Jakob had to sell their company. They had lost a bid to light the city of Munich with electric lights, but they didn't have the money to convert their operations from direct current to the favored alternating current. Following this, the family moved to Italy, while Albert stayed in Munich to continue his studies.

Einstein was going to pursue a degree in electrical engineering but didn't get along well with his teachers. He resented the school's teaching methods and strict regimen and even recommended that the learning should be more creative-based. The authorities would have none of it. With that, the young Albert joined his family in Pavia, Italy.

As a sixteen-year-old in 1895, Einstein took the entrance exams for the Swiss Federal Polytechnic in Zurich, Switzerland. He failed the general portion of the exam but did outstandingly well in mathematics and physics. Instead of the Polytechnic institute, Einstein finished out his secondary education at the Argovian cantonal school in Aarau, Switzerland.

While lodging with one of his professors, Jost Winteler, Einstein fell in love with his daughter, Marie. In 1896, Einstein renounced his German citizenship in order to avoid military service. It was from this point on that Einstein ceased to think of himself as German.

He did well on his high school exam, with top grades in mathematics and physics. At age 17, he enrolled in the four-year program at the Zurich Polytechnic in order to receive a teaching diploma. Marie Winteler, his girlfriend, was also a teacher and moved away to assume a teaching post.

One of the other students at the Polytechnic that year was a young woman named Mileva Maric. Of the six students in the mathematics and physics diploma program, she was the only woman. Einstein and Maric grew closer by studying together, and after a few years, a romance had blossomed. In 1900, Einstein was awarded his teaching diploma, but Maric failed her exams. Nonetheless, she was destined to become Einstein's wife.

Einstein had always been a solitary child; one not given to many friends or schoolmates. But by the time he graduated with his diploma, he was a self-assured, confident and quite talkative young man, who seemed much different from his lonelier early days. His decision to pursue teaching may have come from the reality that his family was in dire need of money after his father's business failed. He was young and was ready to make his mark in the world. Little did he know.

Chapter Two

Einstein's First Endeavors

"The difference between genius and stupidity is; genius has its limits."

—Alexandre Dumas

Einstein was both German and Jewish. But, throughout his lifetime, he never considered himself either one. Germany had been founded on a militaristic philosophy; just before his birth, Bismarck had provoked a war with France which gave him enough proof that the German states needed to band together into one country, which they did in 1870.

All through Einstein's youth, Germany continued its militaristic ways. Bismarck, under Kaiser Wilhelm I, did seem military-mad. This only led to Einstein becoming increasingly disheartened with all Germany stood for.

By the time the year 1900 rolled around, Einstein spent two years looking for a job. Frustrated at every turn, he had approached professors in universities in Europe. Finally, in 1901, he was granted Swiss citizenship; without it, he couldn't hold any teaching post in the country. The downside of the citizenship being that he could have been declared fit for military service, but luckily, he was turned down on the basis of flat feet and varicose veins.

With the help of a friend's father, Einstein secured a position at the Federal Office for Intellectual Property, the patent office in Bern. His new career was that of a level III assistant examiner where he evaluated patent applications for a variety of devices. In 1903, his position became permanent.

Much of what Einstein did at the patent office was scientific. He grappled with questions of electric signals and electrical-mechanical integration of time. Here were two technical problems which would eventually help lead Einstein to conclusions about the nature of light and the connection that existed between space and time.

The patent office work didn't take up much of Einstein's time every day; after all, people were presenting their ideas to him in the hopes of receiving an official Swiss government patent. As long as their invention wasn't copied from someone else's design, it was easy doings for Einstein, especially with his training in engineering and science. This left free hours in the day which Einstein filled up by working on his theories related to physics, and he was able to develop papers on the topic.

For the present, Einstein was happy working at the patent office. Had he found a university position, his believed his creativity would have been squashed. He would have been forced to write up papers which wouldn't have been his best work. Pressures to conform to the prevailing customs of a university would have certainly put the damper on any topics which required his imagination.

Einstein would remain at the patent office for seven years, contented with his work as a patent inspector. It wouldn't be until after he published his papers on relativity, which would revolutionize physics, that he would be offered a position at the university.

By this time, living and working in Bern, Switzerland, Einstein had made the acquaintance of a few friends with whom he would meet on a regular basis. They jokingly called themselves "The Olympia Academy," and they came together to discuss science and philosophy. The other members included Conrad Habicht and Maurice Solovine. Einstein was chosen to be the president of the academy because the group always met in his apartment.

Together this little circle read books from Ernst Mach, John Stuart Mill, David Hume and Spinoza. It was from these treatises that Einstein's philosophies would come. The group itself didn't last long, but the friendships lasted for a lifetime, and so would the profound effects from the readings.

In 1900, Einstein published a paper titled "Conclusions from the Capillarity Phenomena." Capillary action is the ability of a liquid to flow in narrow spaces, without the assistance or the opposition to gravity. This phenomenon was first recorded by Leonardo da Vinci, and it falls under continuum mechanics, which deals with the mechanical behavior of materials.

This was the first paper ever published by Albert Einstein. What happened next would come to astound the scientific world.

Chapter Three

A Tangled Life

"You can't blame gravity for falling in love."

—Albert Einstein

Albert Einstein was to have two wives during his lifetime. While he studied at the Zurich Polytechnic Institute, he had close friends, unlike his solitary upbringing at home. One of these friends was Marcel Grossman, who was one year older than Einstein. Grossman was a top student, and Einstein always relied on his notes when it came time to study for exams. Later on, it would be Grossman who would get him his patent office job, and the same assisted Einstein with his mathematical calculations for his general relativity theory.

Another good friend was Michele Angelo Besso, a mechanical engineer who lived in Zurich. Einstein would join in Besso's musical group, where he would play the violin. Besso encouraged Einstein to read the works of Ernst Mach, a contemporary Austrian philosopher. Mach's philosophies would go a long way in impacting Einstein's special relativity theory.

In these early years at the Institute, Einstein became enamored with his future wife, Mileva Maric. She was Hungarian, and three years older than him. Einstein did have other girlfriends along the way, but it was Maric whom he was drawn to. Maric found herself equally attracted to Einstein, but when she was finished at the Institute, she moved on to Heidelberg University, one of the most famous learning institutions in all of Europe. She wasn't allowed to take classes, but she could sit in on them, and audit them.

Maric wrote Einstein long letters, and eventually, he encouraged her to come back to Zurich, which she did in April 1896. She moved into a room not far from Einstein's, and by then they were considering themselves a genuine couple. By the summer of 1900, their relationship had heated up.

Mileva Maric was a small and frail woman, she walked with a limp from a hip displacement, and she was often in ill health. Einstein's mother was horrified that he had taken up with a girl who was, in her estimation, beneath them and not particularly bright. After all, his mother was hopeful that Einstein would have pursued his relationship with Marie Winteler, but, nothing came of it. Einstein always regarded the young Maric as his equal in intelligence; someone he could partner with and discuss his theories with.

Curiously, when they both sat for their examinations, they received the two lowest grades of everyone. Maric did so bad she didn't qualify for a teaching diploma. She would have to wait a year and take the exams again.

Once graduated, Einstein returned to his family for a visit. His mother Pauline was decidedly opposed to her son marrying someone so beneath him; she called Maric "unwomanly" and "a book," when what her son needed, she insisted, was a wife. Pauline also objected to the union on the grounds that Maric was three years older than Einstein and would shortly become an old hag and a witch.

For some time Einstein was unemployed after getting his diploma from the Institute. He and Maric lived together in her accommodation. During this period, he was receiving letters from his family, asking that he return home. Then, finally, with the aid of his friend Grossman, Einstein secured his position in the patent office.

Just before he took the job, Maric announced she was pregnant. Both she and Einstein felt this was a good thing. Maric's parents encouraged a marriage, but Einstein's parents were violently against one.

Maric once again took the exam to graduate but received the exact same grade as the first time. Here was a young woman who so desperately wanted her degree, but couldn't quite pass the exams. She returned to her family, sad and pregnant. Maric was hoping for an early marriage because if the baby was born illegitimate, it would most likely be put up for adoption. So far, Einstein's family knew nothing of the pregnancy.

Letters were written and sent to Maric and her family from Pauline and Hermann Einstein, declaring their opposition to any marriage ever taking place. Maric was upset and saddened to believe anyone could think that way.

In January 1902, Mileva gave birth to a daughter, Lieserl. Once little Lieserl Einstein was born, her father,

Albert, sent letters asking for details as to what the baby looked like and how Maric was progressing after giving birth.

From this point forward, there was no word of a daughter born to Einstein and Maric. Had the patent office found out, they surely would have terminated Einstein's employment, so secrecy was of the highest regard. The letters between the new parents concerning their daughter were kept hidden. The world never knew of Lieserl until the 1980s. What became of little Lieserl is uncertain; she was most likely adopted by close friends, and then in 1903, she came down with scarlet fever only nineteen months old. It is thought that she died from the illness.

Einstein and Maric were finally married in January 1903. Just before this, Einstein's father was stricken ill while living with his family in Milan, Italy. Einstein loved his parents deeply, even after the trouble they had given him about Mileva, and when his father died at the age of 55, Einstein was tremendously distressed. Adding to this, Maric was never the happy homemaker. She didn't like being a housewife and felt that she had much more to give in scientific circles. However, in May 1904, their son Hans Albert Einstein was born. This birth made his parents ecstatically happy.

It seemed as if the Einsteins were headed for brighter times, what with one son born and Einstein himself procuring a teaching position at the university. By the time the couple was in Prague, they were enjoying a higher standard of living, but Maric continued to feel like an outsider in the country. She was miserable living there.

Maric was infallibly finding cause to be jealous of his relationships with others. Over the years, it is documented that Einstein had numerous affairs. And now that Einstein was a famous scientist, his friends no longer crowded into his living room to discuss theories; his colleagues would discuss things with him in academic settings. This didn't sit well with Maric, who felt like nothing more than a housewife.

One of the people that Einstein was particularly close to was his first cousin Elsa Lowenthal. By 1909, Einstein was a famous personage in the scientific world and was offered a professorship in Zurich. He and Maric were happy to be leaving Bern, and it was about this time that Maric found she was pregnant again.

The Einstein's returned to Zurich and were surrounded by good friends and happy times. In July 1910, a second son Eduard was born. His parents would affectionately call him Tete. When he was a young man, Eduard studied medicine, wanting to become a doctor. However, at the age of 20, he suffered a schizophrenic breakdown. It is not known how severe Eduard's illness was or whether prevailing treatments of the time were doing him any good, but by the time he was in his twenties, he could no longer live by himself. Eduard was committed to an institution where he remained for the rest of his life. His mother would visit him frequently. His father, not so much. By the time Einstein moved permanently to the United States in 1933, he never saw his son again. Eduard would live until 1965.

By 1912, Einstein would return to Berlin for a while, and his marriage was collapsing. It was here that he became involved with his cousin Elsa. Elsa was Einstein's first cousin on his mother's side and second cousin on his father's side. She was also three years older than Einstein, divorced, with two daughters Margot and Ilse.

Despite this, Einstein didn't find it hard to fall in love with Elsa. His marriage to Maric was increasingly challenging, and he sought solace in someone else. In many ways, Elsa was the complete opposite of Maric; sweet, not very educated and loved her role as a housewife. Where once Einstein loved having a partner who was his intellectual equal, now he was looking for someone who didn't have those lofty aspirations.

By the end of 1912, the Einstein family was vastly discontented. The younger son, Hans Albert, could remember the tension between his parents which seemed to grow by the day. Einstein wanted to stay in Prague, but the family ended up in Zurich where they had begun. The whole family appeared to be suffering ailments of one type or another, but Maric was happy to be back in the city she loved most.

Nonetheless, Maric's health problems were getting worse. Her hip ailment was added to by severe rheumatoid arthritis, and she was often in severe pain. Once back in Switzerland, Einstein and Elsa kept in touch through letters. At one point, he even asked her to come to Zurich for what nowadays would be termed a "wild weekend."

At the time, Einstein was offered a full professorship at the University of Berlin, but Maric was understandably unhappy about making a move to Germany. Einstein himself, however, was ecstatic; he would be living in the same city as Elsa. Once the move to Berlin became a reality, the Einstein's marriage rapidly disintegrated.

Einstein was caught up in his academic life, and Maric was left to her own devices. She also managed to have an affair of her own, with a Serbian mathematics professor. Finally, by July of 1914, one month prior to World War I breaking out, the Einsteins' marriage was over.

Maric took the boys and moved in with a good friend in Berlin. She still wanted to get their marriage back on track. Einstein wasn't as willing, but he agreed to stay together for the children, contingent on a list of domestic conditions that he wanted Maric to fulfill. Maric was to launder his clothes, give him three meals a day in his room, leave his room alone, to renounce all relational duties that included going out with friends and all sexual involvement, to not talk to Einstein if he didn't want it, and that she should not belittle or talk against him to their children. Surprisingly, Maric agreed to them all.

Einstein wanted the marriage to end, but Maric didn't seem to grasp his desire. Finally, when he impressed on her that they were to have nothing more than a business relationship, she relented. They agreed to a separation, prior to getting a divorce.

Maric moved back to Zurich, and Einstein sent her money every month for the boys. He was not happy to see his children move so far away, but he did have Elsa waiting patiently for him. Patience was a virtue all women who were involved with Einstein would learn to have.

This time Einstein's mother, Pauline, was overjoyed even though Maric didn't consent to a full divorce initially. It is not known if she knew of the affair between her husband and Elsa, but even if she did, Maric would have known that she had little power in the matter.

By 1916, Elsa was pressuring Einstein to be married. After all, her relatives were all Einsteins too. Finally, that year, Einstein asked Maric for the full divorce. He wished to visit his sons occasionally, and he increased his support for them. In the meantime, illness pre-empted any thoughts of divorce, and it wasn't until the end of the war, that Einstein's marriage would legally end.

Before the court in Zurich, Einstein pled guilty to having committed adultery, so the blame was put on him and not Maric. Once the decree came through, Einstein returned to Germany where six months later he married Elsa in June 1919.

They would stay together through the rest of Einstein's life. They slept in separate bedrooms, but both seemed to enjoy the arrangement. Elsa's daughters lived with them, and she herself was comfortable living in Berlin. She would prove to be a cheerful companion as the years progressed.

In letters that surfaced in 2015, it was revealed that Einstein had written to his former love Marie Winteler in

1910. He admitted he still had strong feelings for her and continued to say that "I think of you in heartfelt love every spare minute and am so unhappy as only a man can be." This was all while his wife Maric was pregnant with their second child. Einstein believed his love was misguided and there was a "missed life" without Marie. Einstein's personal life was indeed a tangled one.

Chapter Four

Living in a Revolutionary Time

"Intelligence is the ability to adapt to change."

—Stephen Hawking

To most of us, if we've seen a photograph of Albert Einstein standing in front of a blackboard covered in mathematical formulas, the equations all looks like Greek. Because of his prominence in the world of numbers and physics, it does seem as if what Einstein is famous for could never be understood by the vast majority of people.

The year 1905 would prove to be a most productive year for Albert Einstein. At the end of April, he completed his thesis and was awarded a Ph.D. from the University of Zurich. His dissertation was entitled "A New Determination of Molecular Dimensions."

Later that year, Einstein would publish four papers that electrified the academic world. One was on the photoelectric effect, the second was about Brownian motion, the third was special relativity and the fourth on the equivalence of mass and energy. He was a mere 26 years old.

Trying to wrap your mind around these four theses is quite a trick, especially if you are not scientifically minded. But Richard Panek, a writer who has received a Guggenheim fellowship and written for many periodicals summed it up best when he said "Over four months, March through June 1905, Albert Einstein produced four papers that revolutionized science. One explained how to measure the size of molecules in a liquid, a second posited how to determine their movement, and a third described how light comes in packets called photons – the foundation of quantum physics and the idea that eventually won him the Nobel Prize. A fourth paper introduced special relativity, leading physicists to reconsider notions of space and time that had sufficed since the dawn of civilization. Then, a few months later, almost as an afterthought, Einstein pointed out in a fifth paper that matter and energy can be interchangeable at the atomic level specifically, that E=mc2, the scientific basis of nuclear energy and the most famous mathematical equation in history."

Keep in mind that at the time Einstein wrote these papers he didn't have Google to help him out. Colleagues available to discuss all of his findings were few and far between, and he didn't even have easy access to scientific reference materials. The Olympian Academy of which Einstein was its star member, and his wife Mileva Maric did have a hand in his writings; how much influence they had is anybody's guess.

The world had barely landed in the 20th century, and the year 1905 was an impressive one worldwide. In the

Russo-Japanese War, Port Arthur surrendered to the Japanese, and the Russians suffered other defeats. The Russian Revolution of 1905 began on "Bloody Sunday" when troops fired into defenseless demonstrators in St. Petersburg. This would lead to more riots and strikes all across the country. The Russian Tsar Nicolas II would try to appease the mobs with little success. This same tsar would be executed along with his entire family in the Russian Revolution in 1918.

In America, the Industrial Workers of the World was founded in Chicago in the hopes of giving more control to labor unions and less to companies. There were now 18-hour train rides from New York to Chicago, and electric lights were beginning to be seen everywhere.

In entertainment, Isadora Duncan started the first school for modern dance in Berlin, Germany and the first movie theater opened in Pittsburgh, Pennsylvania. Pablo Picasso switched from his Blue Period to his Rose Period, and James Joyce completed his first book, *Dubliners*.

Adolf Hitler lived in Vienna and was rejected twice by the Academy of Fine Arts, being told his talents were "unfitness for painting." It would be in Vienna that he would pick up his anti-Semite inclinations. Theodore Roosevelt was inaugurated as the 26th president of the United States and Franklin D. Roosevelt married Teddy's cousin Eleanor.

The Wright Brothers made their first flight in June 1905. The legendary baseball player Ty Cobb faced tragedy when his mother accidentally shot her husband dead when she mistook him for a burglar. All around the globe were strikes and picketing as discontented workers were beginning to see the light of a new day dawning not far away.

It was into this world that Albert Einstein stepped. Walking home from work one day he caught up with a friend Michael Besso, also a physicist working in the patent office. Their discussions led them to a theory put forth by Galileo in 1632, which involved sitting on a dock observing a ship moving along the water. If someone dropped a rock from the top of the mast, where would it land? Would it fall at the base of the mast or further back to correspond to the distance the ship was traveling?

Einstein took this one step further. He asked, what if the object wasn't a rock but a beam of light? Einstein agreed with Galileo that the beam of light would land at the base of the mast. From anyone sitting and observing on the dock, the base of the mast will have moved out from the top of the mast during the light's descent; from the sitter's point of view, the distance the light has traveled has lengthened.

Einstein posited that the speed of light is always 186,282 miles per second. Speed is nothing more than distance divided by a length of time. So, when you are observing a beam of light, the speed will always be 186,282 miles per second. If you change the distance that the light travels, you have to modify the time.

How do you change time? According to Einstein, time is not constant. Suddenly it becomes a variable, depending on many factors; how you and whatever you're observing move in relation to each other. No longer would the universal clock that kept time for all to observe, be true.

If you were sitting on the dock and watching the light beam, it would take longer than a second to go from the top of the mast to the base. This looked like the time on board the ship was passing more slowly than on the dock. In order for this to be entirely true, the reverse would have to work as well. For a sailor on the ship observing a beam of light sent from, say, a tall building on land, it would appear to the sailor that the light travels farther than you saw on the dock. The sailor would observe that time was passing slower on the dock than on the ship.

And so, there was the new principle of relativity. Viewing space by itself and time by itself would begin to fall by the wayside. All that separates the two is math. Einstein knew that these ideas or perceptions were all we could ever fathom in the world. That being true, they were all we could ever know. As far as the measure of the universe was concerned, they were all that mattered.

Einstein would stay at the patent office until 1909, but he was getting to be well known at this point. By 1906, some of the most prominent scientists in Germany were debating his work.

Only two years later, Einstein was recognized as a leader in the scientific world, and he became a lecturer at the University of Bern. The following year he gave a lecture on electrodynamics and his new relativity principle. Alfred Kleiner, a physicist at the University of Zurich, wanted him to join the faculty at the university. A newly created professorship in theoretical physics was offered to Einstein. He was appointed as an associate professor in 1909.

In April 1911, Einstein became a professor at the Charles-Ferdinand University in Prague. In order to do this, he accepted Austrian citizenship. He wrote 11 scientific works while there. In 1912, he returned to Zurich once again. For the next two years, he was a professor of theoretical physics; he also studied continuum mechanics, the problem of gravitation and the molecular theory of heat.

By 1914, Einstein returned to the German Empire, where he was now director of the Kaiser Wilhelm Institute for Physics, and he was also a member of the Humbolt University in Berlin. By this time Einstein's marriage to Mileva Maric was at an end, and she would move back to Zurich with the children.

Einstein was relieved as he had another lover waiting in the wings, but at the same time, he was quite sad to see his sons go and wept after they boarded the train to Switzerland. He would see them just a few times each year and never in a home where his second wife Elsa, would be present.

At this point, Einstein's happiness seems to have flown out the window. With his marriage in shambles, he and his ex-wife communicated back and forth through letters all about money, property rights, and custody. Then World War I erupted in late summer of 1914. Berlin was not the best of places to find oneself in at the onset of war.

Einstein did not support the war; he was a socialist, an internationalist, and a pacifist. Some of his friends would go on to develop bombs and poison gases for the German army. This horrified Einstein who wrote a lengthy treatise on pacifism. It was never published.

During the war, while Europe was disintegrating all around him, Einstein busied himself with studying his special relativity theory. He presented his findings in November of 1915. His theory of space-time would overturn what the scientific world had known since the time of Isaac Newton. Einstein's new model created the basis for modern physics of today.

For the rest of the war, Einstein was also working on dissolving his marriage to Maric once and for all. He was eager to move on with his life, but it would take time before both Einstein and Maric would come to a final agreement on money and future wealth.

In June 1919, he and Elsa were married at last. Her two daughters came to live with them, and life seemed untroubled again. The war was over, and people all around the world recognized Albert Einstein as a genius scientist; one who would continue to amaze the world.

In 1911, Einstein had proposed that light from another star should be bent by the sun's gravity. This would be proven right in 1919, by Sir Arthur Eddington in an eclipse of the sun on May 29. When these observations were published, they made Einstein world famous.

The London Times had published a headline declaring: "Revolution in Science – New Theory of the Universe – Newtonian Ideas Overthrown." All based on the theories of Albert Einstein. It seemed as if there was nothing this man couldn't imagine.

Chapter Five

Traveling Abroad

"I believe anyone can conquer fear by doing the things he fears to do, provided he keeps doing them until he gets a record of successful experience behind him."

—Eleanor Roosevelt

By the time World War I had come to a close, Albert Einstein was a well-known name around the world in scientific circles. For years he had complained that his work was not bringing him the recognition he desired, and now that it had, he complained that the press, among others, wouldn't leave him be.

Germany had been crushed into the ground by 1918. Its peoples were demoralized, there was a massive debt hanging over them, and the way forward seemed almost impossible to fathom. Most people ran their lives on everyday order and routine, trying to fit Einstein's physics into it held no interest for them. Even though he wasn't a practicing Jew, he was regarded as someone of the Jewish faith, and with that recognition came all the anti-Semitism people could throw his way.

Einstein, as he himself said, stood for no nation or religion. He was one of the first globalists, believing in international laws to make the world right. But, as the

1920s rolled on, many Jewish people were trying to dispel the idea of their Jewishness, and this made Einstein talk about his Jewishness all the more.

In 1921, Einstein visited New York City for the first time. He was welcomed by the mayor and then spent three weeks lecturing and attending receptions. He was quite taken with how joyous Americans were towards life, and he would write about this in a future publication. Einstein also visited Princeton during this stay, a place he would come to call home a decade later. Just as he had predicted to Maric, in 1922 Einstein won the Nobel Prize in physics.

That same year Einstein visited Asia, where he stopped in places like Singapore, Sri Lanka, and Japan. In the latter, he gave lectures before thousands of people. While he was traveling in the Far East, he wasn't able to personally accept the Nobel Prize; in his place was a German diplomat who praised Einstein not only for his scientific views but for his international and activist peacekeeping ways.

On his return to Europe, Einstein stopped in Palestine. He was greeted by their head of state, and ordinary citizens were excited to see him; even storming a building he was in, wanting to hear him speak. He praised the people, saying how happy it was making him that the Jewish people were finally being recognized.

During the 1920s Einstein's family life, on the other hand, was not all that happy. Besides his own indiscretions, Einstein was wretched with his son Hans Albert's choice for a wife. Then, his younger son Eduard tried to commit suicide and had to be institutionalized.

As the decade was drawing to a close, Einstein was not contributing to the world of science anymore, so much as he involved himself in the politics of the day. It was during these heady days that socialism and fascism were poised to make a comeback on the European stage. Einstein cared for neither socialism or fascism nor any other ideological government system. He called himself a "militant pacifist" and would not regard nationalism as worthy of his time. This led communist supporters to look for his aid in their local rebellions. He always said that intellectual freedom could never operate under beliefs in doctrinal governments.

In 1930, Einstein made a second visit to America. Once the word got out that Einstein was back in the U.S., it seemed like everyone wanted to see him and meet with him. He declined every invitation. Einstein arrived in New York City where he was given the keys to the city by Mayor Jimmy Walker. He visited Chinatown, the Metropolitan Opera, Columbia University, and Madison Square Garden, where he took part in a large Hanukkah celebration.

Then Einstein traveled to southern California. The visit was planned for two months, to give Einstein enough time to do research at the California Institute of Technology. However, he didn't get along well with a noted scientist there due to his pacifist ways, even telling students that science was often inclined to do more harm than good.

It was at this time that Einstein visited Universal Studios where he met with Charlie Chaplin, an actor known for his pacifism. Einstein and Chaplin took an instant liking to each other. One of Chaplin's movies, City Lights, was having its premiere in a few days, and he invited Einstein and Elsa to the opening. In the new era of celebrity, this was a photo shoot for the ages.

By the early 1930s, new things were brewing on the world horizon. Germany would play a significant role—as would Albert Einstein.

Chapter Six

Becoming American

"Genius is one percent inspiration and ninety-nine percent perspiration."

—Thomas Edison

By June 1932, Einstein was offered a chance to join the faculty at Princeton University. Oxford and Caltech had offered him positions prior to this; he was still mulling them over. With the uprising of one Adolf Hitler, Einstein's family knew he would have to make up his mind soon, and fast.

In December, Einstein, along with over 30 pieces of luggage, sailed for America aboard the ship Oakland. One month later, Hitler became Chancellor of Germany, and three months later he would give himself the infamous name of "fuhrer." A dictatorship was now taking over Germany.

Upon hearing this, Einstein turned in his passport and renounced his German citizenship for the second time in his life.

In 1933, Einstein and Elsa traveled to Europe, going to Belgium. It was there they learned that Einstein's cottage had been raided by the Nazis and his sailboat had been confiscated. A few years later, the Nazis turned his cabin into a Hitler Youth Camp.

Traveling to Switzerland, Einstein and Elsa stopped at the home of his ex-wife Mileva. Einstein had come a long way in making things right with his first wife; she even invited them to stay with her while in Switzerland. Einstein believed that even when he was living in the U.S., he would make yearly visits to Europe. However, when he left Europe in October of 1933, it was for the last time. Einstein would never see Europe again.

He would take up a position at Princeton at the Institute for Advanced Study. This institute was a haven for scientists like Einstein who had fled Nazi Germany. Einstein still was not set on where he would permanently settle. He had offers from universities in Europe and the U.S. By 1935 he decided to stay in America for good. It was at this time that he applied for American citizenship.

The Einsteins enjoyed their time in America. Of course being a noted scientific celebrity was all to the good, but Einstein looked on the American people as more diverse and less anti-Semitic than the ravings that were going on in Europe at the time.

Unfortunately, misfortune struck the Einsteins beginning in 1934. Elsa's daughter Ilse died, and her other daughter Margot moved to New Jersey to be with her mother. In 1936, Elsa herself became ill with kidney problems. She seemed to rally a bit while on vacation in the Adirondack Mountains, but by December, she was failing and died before the year was out.

Einstein was quite grief-stricken by her death. He wouldn't see anyone, even though his close circle of friends would try to encourage him to leave the house. Eventually, his sister Maja, with whom he had been near all his life, moved from Italy to join him in America. She had more than one reason to leave Italy, as Mussolini had come to power and was threatening the Jews there.

Just before the start of World War II, Hans Albert, Einstein's older son, also joined him in America, taking a professorship at Clemson University in South Carolina. Einstein made several attempts to get his younger son Eduard moved to the States, but because he was mentally ill, authorities wouldn't allow him to come.

Einstein would remain at the Institute for Advanced Study until his death in 1955. As time went by, Einstein was a staunch supporter for pointing out the errors of socialism and fascism. In the early 1930s, Einstein believed that Hitler would come to rue the day he had driven all the scientists out of Germany. Little did he know how right he would be.

In time, by 1939, word was out that the Nazis were trying to develop an atomic bomb. At the time no one paid this group of Hungarian scientists any mind. Einstein along with another physicist who had immigrated to America, Leo Szilard, took it upon themselves to alert the officials in Washington D.C. to the dangers of what the Nazi regime was up to. At first, no one paid them any attention, but as the war dragged on, minds began to change.

Chapter Seven

WWII and The Manhattan Project

"Peace cannot be kept by force; it can only be achieved by understanding."

—Albert Einstein

Even before the war began, there were hints that the Nazi's were up to no good. They had driven the Jews out of Germany or into hiding by 1939, and those who had waited until then to go were finding it impossible. Subsequently, the threat of an atomic bomb loomed in the distance.

In July, two months before the war was officially underway, the Hungarian scientists, Szilard and Wigner visited Einstein to explain how do-able the bomb would be for the Germans. They asked for his support in writing a letter to President Roosevelt and top Washington officials, recommending that the U.S. start paying attention to the Nazi's and that America should begin its own nuclear weapons research.

Roosevelt knew he could not risk letting Hitler get an atomic bomb first. Because of Einstein's letter and his meetings with the president, suddenly the race was on; to develop a nuclear weapon before any other country. After all, the U.S. had immense financial and material resources, not to mention a well-established scientific community.

This would be known as the Manhattan Project. In 1938, two German scientists had discovered nuclear fission, which made the development of an atomic bomb theoretically possible. The project was under the direction of Major General Leslie Groves of the U.S. Army Corp of Engineers, and J. Robert Oppenheimer directed the entire project.

The United States became the only country to develop nuclear weapons successfully during World War II and was the only country ever to use them. Two atomic bombs were eventually unleashed in Japan, one on Hiroshima on August 6, and one on Nagasaki on August 9, 1945. This act would officially bring WWII to its close.

Einstein being a pacifist, called war a disease. He knew when signing the letter that went to President Roosevelt that he was going against his principles. One good thing did come out of the war years for Einstein. In 1940, he became an American citizen. He recognized in American culture the ideals of creativity and freedom, which were two he valued since his childhood.

Chapter Eight

Einstein's Beliefs

"I fear the day that technology will surpass our human interaction. The world will have a generation of idiots."

—Albert Einstein

Most people remember Albert Einstein for his scientific contributions. Yet, he was much more than that. There were causes and passions in his life that went far beyond elementary particles and gravitational field equations. Take his love of music, for instance. This was fostered in the young Einstein by his mother who played the piano rather well. She wanted Einstein to learn the violin which he did. By the time he was 13 years old, Einstein had discovered Mozart's violin sonatas. He loved Mozart's music so much that he was inspired to become a better violinist.

For all of his life, Einstein loved music. He always said had he not been a physicist, he would have been a musician. Einstein said he would think and daydream in music. All the while when living in Switzerland, he would get together with other musicians, and they would play together. Einstein was quite remarkable at playing the violin.

Another area of his life which he was passionate about was racism. He even considered racism to be America's "worst disease." Einstein hated racism so much he even became a member of the NAACP while living in Princeton. Einstein visited a black college in Pennsylvania and was awarded an honorary degree. It was said that he paid the college tuition for a black student.

In addition to racism causes, Einstein assisted in many Zionist causes. This was rather peculiar, noting how he was never a practicing Jew. He did help to establish the Hebrew University of Jerusalem in 1925 and was on its Board of Governors. Once the state of Israel was created, Chaim Weizmann, who would later be Israel's first president, offered Einstein the position of President of Israel, a mostly ceremonial post. This was in 1952 and Einstein declined, writing that he was deeply moved, but he could not accept it.

Einstein, during his lifetime, was unwavering in favor of socialism and critical of capitalism. Known as a man who was constantly being called upon to give his opinions and hypotheses on all things mathematical and having to do with physics, Einstein strongly advocated for a democratic global government. He believed that a world federation would hold nation-states in check correctly.

As far as his religious views were concerned, Einstein wrote about them in many original writings and also did interviews discussing them. Einstein stated that he did not believe in a personal God who intervenes for people or circumstances, something he believed was a naive point of view.

Einstein was not an atheist, but he did refer to himself as an agnostic. He also said he was a "deeply religious nonbeliever." He also did not believe in an afterlife, stating that "one life is enough for me."

Chapter Nine

Later Life and Death

"Towering genius disdains a beaten path. It seeks regions hitherto unexplored."

—Abraham Lincoln

At the age of 66, Einstein retired from public life. It was 1948. He still came to his office in Princeton every day, and of course, if you were lucky enough to run into him in the halls or on the grounds, it was a memorable experience.

In that same year, his first wife Mileva Maric fell on the ice, lapsed into a coma and died months later. Einstein had promised himself that he would take care of Eduard, even if it bankrupted him. Maric, after all, had devoted her life to taking care of her younger son in the institution.

Soon after Maric's death, Einstein began suffering health problems as well. During surgery, it was revealed that he was afflicted by an aneurysm in his abdominal aorta. At the time, there was nothing that could be done for such an ailment, and Einstein knew that the aneurysm could burst at any time and kill him. With proper diet and rest, he could live some years, but his fate was sealed.

His wife was gone, his sister too had died. Still, Einstein was surrounded by many friends and colleagues in his final years. He also had his step-daughter Margot and his longtime secretary, Helen Dukas.

By 1955, Einstein had become quite ill. When he heard that his good friend Michael Besso had died, he believed his time was short. He was 76 years old. In April, the aortic aneurysm began to rupture. Einstein collapsed at home and was in a lot of pain, which was managed with morphine. When he could no longer stand the pain, Einstein was taken to the hospital. His son flew in to be with him, family and friends were near. He actually rallied for a bit, taking with him notes that he was preparing for a speech he would give commemorating the State of Israel's seventh anniversary. Unfortunately, he didn't live long enough to finish it.

Einstein died in the early morning hours of April 18, 1955. The aneurysm burst, and he died instantly. He was cremated and his ashes scattered, so there would be no memorial for people to visit. Thomas Harvey, the coroner, removed his brain prior to the cremation for study, without permission from the family. Hans Albert finally relented to the request to not cremate the brain.

Einstein's brain remained with Harvey at the Princeton labs until 1998. Pieces of it was given to scientists who had asked for it. As far as any research on Einstein's brain, there was nothing of significance. Einstein would have understood. He always claimed there was nothing special about him, only his love for curiosity.

Chapter Ten

The Legacy of Albert Einstein

"The ones who are crazy enough to think that they can change the world, are the ones who do."

—Steve Jobs

Nowadays, Albert Einstein is a household name. Almost everyone recognizes his face, and Einstein has come to be a synonym for genius. Many decades have passed since his death, and his theories were formulated more than a century ago, yet Einstein continues to fascinate. Many others than scientists marvel at all Albert Einstein was.

It does appear to be that Einstein showed up in history right when he was needed. His general and special relativity theories absolutely stood the world on its head. Add to that the fact that in the early 20th century the whole world was changing, and Einstein seemed to be setting the stage for the rest.

It was truly a time of transformation. Freudian psychology was new to the scene, but Einstein would never allow himself to be affected by it. He wouldn't, so to speak, put himself on the couch. As a baby, he took his time learning to speak. Some still say that Einstein was a slow learner.

Slow learner or not, what that did was to make Einstein curious about the world around him. It was all of his curiosity about such things as space and time which would make such an impact on the world. Some researchers claim Einstein was autistic because of his learning patterns, yet by his teen years, Einstein had lots of friends and enjoyed himself amidst the discussions and relationships just like anyone else.

One thing people often think they know about Albert Einstein is that he, too, failed in math class. While at Princeton in 1935, a rabbi had shown him a clipping with the headline "Greatest living mathematician failed in mathematics." Einstein told the rabbi he had never failed in math. In fact, by the time he was fifteen years old he had mastered differential and integral calculus. His parents would buy him math textbooks so he could continue learning over the summer months. This, of course, led him to try to prove new theories by going at them himself.

There is only a handful of monumental scientists in history; Charles Darwin, Isaac Newton, and Albert Einstein were three of them. No one surpassed them. Of Einstein, there are those who believe his discoveries were merely theoretical in nature. Yet, all of his revelations have generated many practical applications.

All of the great findings of the 20th century would never have been achieved without the influence of Albert Einstein. Modern physics would not have advanced to where it is today; speaking of cosmology, quantum theory, and relativity. Einstein's contributions to these fields were greater than any other scientist, ever.

Even today there are parts of his discoveries that are left unfinished. The structure of quantum mechanics, for instance, is still not properly defined and it was something which never satisfied Einstein in his day.

And what would Einstein think of all this? Although he will forever be hailed as the most brilliant mathematical physicist of the 20th century, he regarded himself as more of a philosopher than a scientist. It was Einstein whose legacy points to space and time being woven into one fabric. He would tell you that it is matter which causes space-time to curve, and that motion and properties are altered in their turn, by this curvature. Who thinks like this except Albert Einstein?

Culturally speaking, what Einstein did for physics could also be applied to what was happening in the world in which he lived. Up until that magic year of 1905, all laws of the universe were based on the theories of Isaac Newton. These were mechanical in nature and based on absolute laws and certainties. These laws had ushered in the Enlightenment and all of the social upheaval which went with it.

Then along comes Albert Einstein with an entirely new vision. Here was a view of the universe where space and time were dependent on certain frames of reference. Gone were Newton's certainties, in its place were now theories which seemed almost godless. This was imaginative nonconformity at its apex; what it did for morality, politics, art and science can be read about in the history books.

Best of all, we still live in Einstein's universe. This man was able to envision everything unseen, from the smallest to the largest. His sweep of modern science went from the infinitesimal to the infinite; from the smallest of photons to the greatest events, where the cosmos is still expanding and never-ending. Think of all the things that are known of in modern life; television, semiconductors, space travel, nuclear power, photoelectric cells, lasers and so much more; these are directly connected to Albert Einstein.

Einstein knew that in order to flourish and grow in life, one must be free. He came to understand and to love America's freedoms, for he saw in them the best way for people to express themselves. He always believed that the pre-eminent approach to learning was through imagination; that with these pictures in your brain your creativity would be set free.

In his last days, he was working on a speech that he was scheduled to give for Israeli Independence Day. "I speak to you today not as an American citizen and not as a Jew, but as a human being." He never finished it. Einstein picked up a little notebook of numbers and calculations instead, which he was hoping would lead him to a better world than the one he was leaving.

Perhaps he found that better world on the other side. Either way, what Albert Einstein gave to the world was more than incredible. The laws of the universe were waiting for him. In his spirit, his legacy goes before him.

Conclusion

Albert Einstein stands as the 20th century's most brilliant mind. His face and his thick accent have been caricatured in numerous movies and entertainment venues. After all, who wouldn't recognize him? He did have a resemblance to a bumbling professor, yet people worldwide flocked to him.

Einstein took what everyone else had thought to be two different scenarios of nature and turned that idea on its head. He viewed them both as equivalent. In his lifetime, Albert Einstein published over 300 scientific papers and 150 non-scientific papers. In 2014, Einstein's papers were released from universities and archives worldwide. They totaled over 30,000 documents.

Einstein wrote on general relativity, and the equivalence principle, special relativity, the photoelectric effect, photons and energy quanta, thermodynamic fluctuations, quantized atomic vibrations, wave-particle duality, gravitational waves, hole argument and Entwurf theory, physical cosmology, modern quantum theory, Bose-Einstein statistics, wormholes, equations of motion, unified field theory and more.

How did his mind work? What made Einstein so different from the masses? How did his scientific theories come to be? Where did his notions about creativity, freedom, and imagination meet?

If you think Albert Einstein is best relegated to another time and place, think again. His theories and inventions are what power today's technologies. Science is a very ennobling endeavor, but without the other things that make us human—love of music, art, relationships—the human world would soon pass away.

What makes Albert Einstein dynamic is that much of his work was the inspiration for so many other things. In the world of art, for instance, Cubism introduced a shifting or relative point of view. Because of Einstein's notion of a four-dimensional space-time, this led some artists to begin looking for a fourth dimension that would result in a higher unity for all peoples.

As Edison had influenced how research laboratories were set up, Einstein believed that his scientific endeavors should be viewed as those which held a moral responsibility to humanity. He believed in pacifism, human dignity, and a life worth living for every person. Each and every scientist should be deeply concerned with not only their theories but how those ideas would impact the world.

To be successful, Einstein believed, one must question authority. Never be content with what is if you can make it better. Creativity is what makes the man and the woman. Einstein ushered in the modern age; now it's time for us to live in it.

Printed in Great Britain
by Amazon

28208251R00029